First Lessons® Bass

By Jay Farmer

Online Audio & Video

Audio
www.melbay.com/99933BCDEB
Video
dv.melbay.com/99933
You Tube
www.melbay.com/99933V

It doesn't get any easier.....

1 2 3 4 5 6 7 8 9 0

Table of Contents

Introduction

The purpose of this book is to introduce beginning bass students to the fundamental concepts of electric bass playing. The material covered in this book is approximately the material covered in the first 8 lessons of private bass instruction. This book is designed to focus on 3 areas: establishing a good left hand position, reading standard bass clef notation, and learning the application of functional bass lines.

The concepts presented in this book are not hard, but they should be practiced slowly and thoroughly before moving on to the next section. In other words, take your time in absorbing all new material presented in each section. Establish good practice habits early in your studies. Space your practice time out over the course of a week. You will get more accomplished by practicing 20 minutes a day 5 days a week rather than trying to cram an hour and a half worth of practice into one day. Also, break your daily practice up into smaller 5 to 10 minute segments. The smaller segments will prevent both physical fatigue and mental fatigue. Returning to an exercise 3 or 4 times a day will help to engrain good habits as your technique begins to develop.

The play-along audio recording will allow you to hear selected exercises as well as play along with the recorded tracks. The bass is recorded only on the *right channel* so that you can turn the recorded bass off and play along by yourself simply by panning left. Be sure to tune your bass to the audio using the tuning notes provided at the begining of the audio. The tuning notes are the open strings presented from highest to lowest: G, D, A, E.

I would like to take this opportunity to thank Rusty Holloway, David Slack, Mike Bearman and Corey Christiansen for their advice and guidance in the writing of this book.

Parts of the Bass

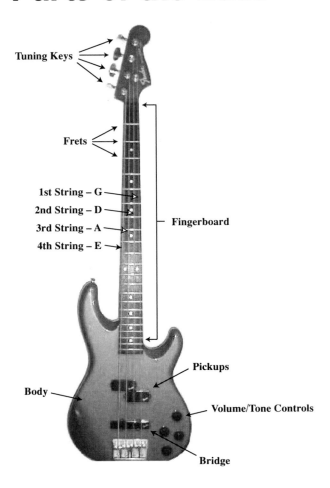

Tuning the Bass

- Tuning using an electronic tuner: Tuners are the fastest and easiest way to tune. Plug the bass into the tuner and a needle and/or a light will indicate which direction to tune the string (higher or lower).

- Tuning using a piano/keyboard: The 4 open strings on the bass can be tuned to a piano or keyboard by locating the notes using the following illustration:

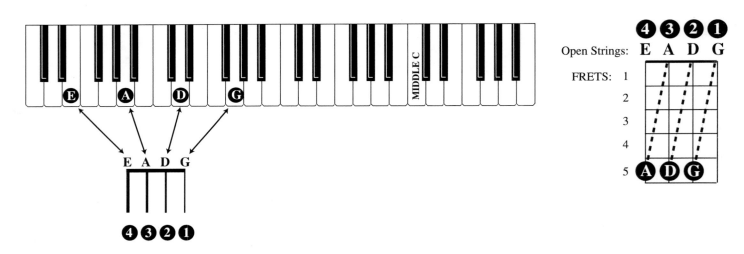

- Relative Tuning: Assuming the 4th string to be in tune, tune the 3rd string to the note played at the fifth fret on the 4th string. Tune the 2nd string to the note at the 5th fret on the 3rd string. Tune the 1st string to the note at the 5th fret on the 2nd string.

The Left Hand Position

It is important to establish good left hand technique. A proper left hand position is important for two reasons:

- To reduce unnecessary wear and tear on your hand
- To establish a systematic approach to the fingerboard

Finger Numberings - The Three Finger System

On the guitar, it is quite easy to space the fingers one finger per fret using four fingers to cover four frets; however, when the same approach is applied to the bass some problems arise. Simply put, the bass is much bigger than a guitar. The strings are bigger, the neck is bigger, the frets are bigger, the body is bigger, the fingerboard is longer... you get the picture! The natural width (without stretching) of the left hand spans three frets on almost all electric basses. We will use this natural width to our advantage. The third and fourth fingers are the weakest fingers of the left hand; therefore, they are coupled together on one fret. The third and fourth fingers are considered one finger and will be collectively referred to as **"4th finger."** Although the third and fourth fingers are coupled together, this does not mean that they have to physically touch each other, they simply work together on the same fret.

The index finger is the **"1st finger."**

The middle finger is the **"2nd finger."**

Shaping the Left Hand Position

Follow these guidelines when forming the left hand position:

- The thumb is placed in the center of the back of the neck (straight up and down, not sideways). The thumb should be lined up with second finger, placing it in the center of the hand position. The thumb is turned on its side so that the corner of the fingertip is in contact with the back of the neck.

- The first finger is placed on the string straight and slightly on its side.

- The second finger is curved so that the fingertip is used to press the string down. To curve the finger, simply bend the finger at both knuckles.

- The fourth finger *(remember: **third and fourth fingers are used together as fourth finger**)* is also curved so that the fingertips are used to press the string down.

In order to maintain a proper three-fret spacing in the left hand, a "V" shape space should exist between the *1st* and the *2nd finger* and between the *2nd* and the *4th finger*. The "V" between the 1st finger and 2nd finger is wider than the "V" between 2nd and 4th fingers.

Using the Hand Position

The hand position should remain relaxed with very little tension in the left hand and forearm. Do not grip the neck of the bass. You will find that it does not take that much pressure to press a string down as long as you *stay on your fingertips!*

- When you are playing 4th finger, the 2nd finger and 1st finger remain on that same string.

- To play 2nd finger, simply lift 4th finger straight up to allow 2nd finger to be played.

- To play 1st finger, lift both 4th finger and 2nd finger to allow 1st finger to be played.

Playing 1st Finger   Playing 2nd Finger   Playing 4th Finger

Keep your fingers close to the fingerboard when they are not being used. Do not let your hand position collapse when you lift your fingers off the string. Always maintain proper spacing between your fingers. **The goal is to have a minimal amount of motion in the left hand. Remember to <u>KEEP YOUR HAND RELAXED!</u>**

Right Hand

The first and second fingers of the right hand are used to pluck the strings. The thumb is placed on the top of one of the pickups. This acts as an anchor to the right hand and will prove to be helpful when dealing with right hand string crossings.

It is important to build independence between 1st and 2nd fingers in the right hand. Practice alternating between 1st and 2nd fingers on an open string. Once you feel comfortable on a single open string, try moving to the next open string. Eventually you should be able to move freely between all four strings, alternating fingers without looking at your right hand.

Positioning the Bass

The position of the bass is similar for both standing and sitting:

- The neck should remain directly to your left side (only slightly tilted up), do not push the neck of the bass away from your body.

- Your elbow should hang freely at your side, do not tuck the elbow into your side or rest the elbow on your thigh.

- When playing in a sitting position, be sure to sit up straight and maintain good posture. Also, it is a good idea to wear a strap even if you are sitting down.

Fundamentals of Music

The **musical alphabet** consists of the first seven letters of the English alphabet:

A – B – C – D – E – F - G

The musical alphabet is cyclical. After the letter G, the next letter is A, starting the cycle over again: A-B-C-D-E-F-G-A-B-C-D-E-F-G-A-B and so on.

Music is written down on a system of 5 lines and 4 spaces called a **staff**. A **clef sign** identifies the names of the lines and spaces. Electric bass music is written in **bass clef**. The names of the lines and spaces of the bass clef are as follows:

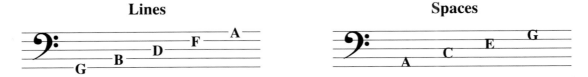

The staff is divided into linear segments called **measures**. Vertical lines indicate the beginning and end of each measure. These lines are called **bar lines**.

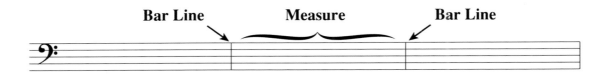

Pitches are represented on the staff by **notes**. There are three parts to a note:

Ledger lines are the short horizontal lines that sometimes appear above or below the staff. Ledger lines extend the range of the staff. When using ledger lines, the notes continue above or below the staff in alphabetical order.

An *interval* is the distance between 2 notes. The smallest interval or distance between 2 notes is a *half step*. On the electric bass, the frets divide the fingerboard into half steps. For example, if you moved from the 1st fret to the 2nd fret on the 4th string, you have moved a half step. A *whole step* is the same as moving the distance of 2 half steps. The distance from the 1st to the 3rd fret is a whole step.

Accidentals are symbols that appear in front of a note.

A *sharp* (♯) raises a note a half step.

A *flat* (♭) lowers a note a half step.

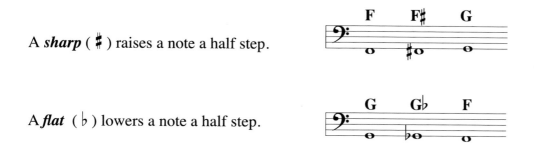

Notice in the example above that the notes F♯ and G♭ exist on the same fret, they are called *enharmonic notes*. Enharmonic notes sound the same but have 2 different names.

A *natural sign* (♮) cancels any preceding sharp or flat.

Note Values

The steady pulse in music is called the **beat**. Note values determine how long a note is going to last. Here are the 4 most common note values used in this book:

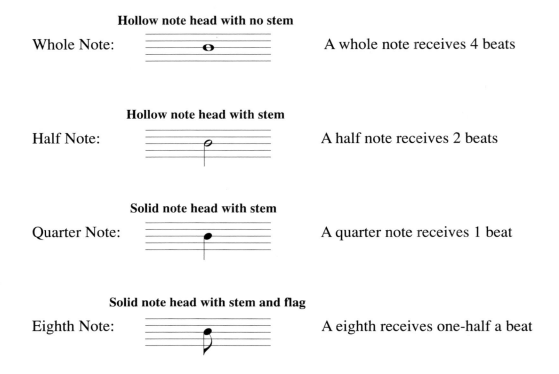

	Hollow note head with no stem	
Whole Note:		A whole note receives 4 beats
	Hollow note head with stem	
Half Note:		A half note receives 2 beats
	Solid note head with stem	
Quarter Note:		A quarter note receives 1 beat
	Solid note head with stem and flag	
Eighth Note:		A eighth receives one-half a beat

Practicing with a Metronome

A metronome is a device that marks a steady beat through a series of clicks, beeps and/or flashing light. Practicing with a metronome is an easy way to keep track of different note values: a whole note will last for 4 clicks; a half note - 2 clicks; quarter note - 1 click. An inexpensive metronome is a valuable tool in developing rhythmic accuracy.

Rests

Just as note values indicate how long a note should last, rest values indicate how long a silence should last. There are 4 corresponding rest values for each of the note values already learned.

	Hangs from the fourth line	
Whole Rest:		A whole rest indicates 4 beats of silence.
	Lays on top of the third line	
Half Rest:		A half rest indicates 2 beats of silence.
Quarter Rest:		A quarter rest indicates 1 beat of silence.

Eighth Rest: An eighth rest indicates a 1/2 beat of silence.

The ***time signature*** determines how many beats will be in a measure. The time signature appears in the staff at the beginning of a line of music. The time signature consists of two numbers stacked on top of each other. The top number indicates how many beats are in a measure; the bottom number tells which note value represents the pulse. Here are the three different time signatures used in this book:

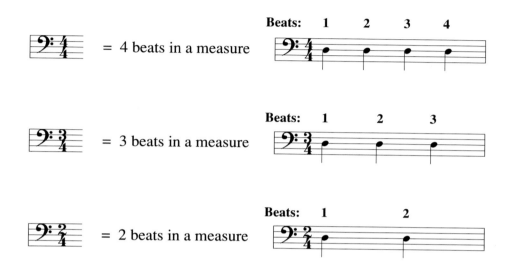

Clap or sing the following examples:

The Open Strings

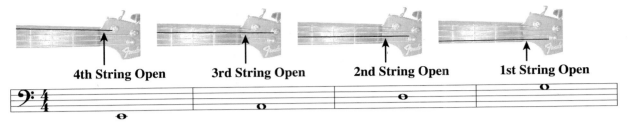

4th String Open   3rd String Open   2nd String Open   1st String Open

Practice the following exercises on the open strings.   Remember to alternate the right hand fingers.

Open String Exercises

Notes on the 4ᵗʰ String

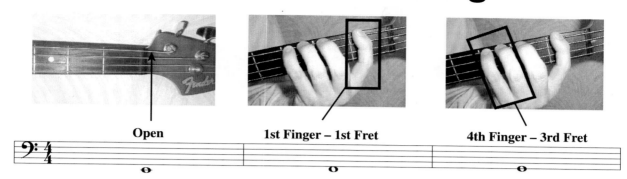

Open　　　　　**1st Finger – 1st Fret**　　　　　**4th Finger – 3rd Fret**

Exercises on the 4ᵗʰ String

Notes on the 3rd String

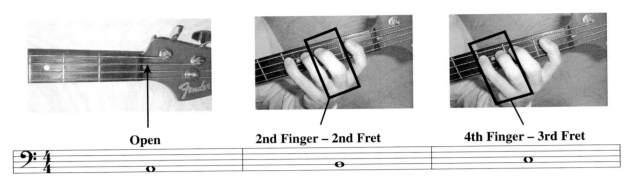

Open   2nd Finger – 2nd Fret   4th Finger – 3rd Fret

Exercises on the 3rd String

Connecting the 3rd and 4th Strings

Theme and Variations

CD#4

Strollin'

CD#5

Bottom Out

CD#6

A Minor Line

CD#7

15

More Music Fundamentals

Eighth Notes

An eighth note receives a half a beat. Two eighth notes are equal to one (1) quarter note.

Two or more eighth notes may be connected by a beam. When counting eighth notes the word "and" is used to mark the 2nd eighth note of the beat.

Compare the relationship between eighth notes and eighth rests with quarter notes:

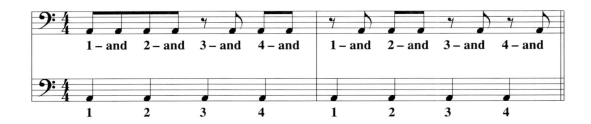

Ties

A **tie** is a curved line connecting two note heads to each other. The tie indicates that the first note is to be held through the time value of the second note. The second note is not played separately. Ties are often used to sustain a note across the bar line.

Repeat Signs

A **repeat sign** consists of two dots before or after two bar lines:

The repeat signs appear at the beginning and the end of the measures that are to be repeated.

When the repeat sign only appears at the end of a section, the section is repeated from the first measure.

16

Notes on the 2ⁿᵈ String

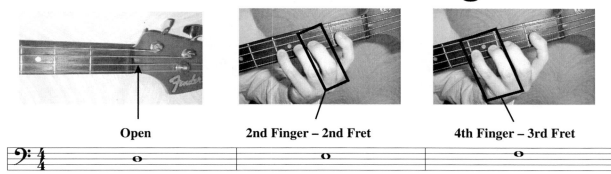

Open   2nd Finger – 2nd Fret   4th Finger – 3rd Fret

Exercises on the 2ⁿᵈ String

Playing in ¾ Time

¾ has three beats in a measure.

When a dot (.) is added to a note, the note's value is increased by one-half.

The dotted-half note (𝅗𝅥.) is sustained for 3 beats:

17

Notes on the 1st String

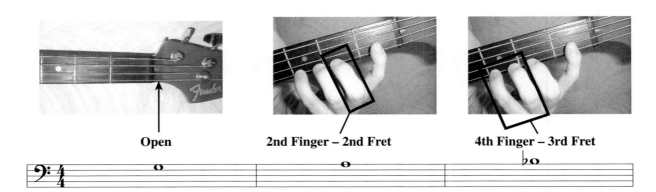

Open   2nd Finger – 2nd Fret   4th Finger – 3rd Fret

Exercises on the 1st String

Connecting the 1st and 2nd Strings

Connecting all Four Strings

Ode to Joy

The Irish Washerwoman

Simple Gifts

BMR 2000

Motion

Journeyesque

21

The First Five Frets

We will now go back and learn the notes that were skipped on each of the four strings.

	1st Fret	2nd Fret	3rd Fret	3rd Fret	2nd Fret	1st Fret
4th String	F	F♯	G	G	G♭	F
3rd String	A♯	B	C	C	B	B♭
2nd String	D♯	E	F	F	E	E♭
1st String	G♯	A	B♭	B♭	A	A♭

Shifting

A shift is simply the process of moving the left hand position from one position on the fingerboard to another. The left hand position moves **as one unit** during a shift. It is important to keep the fingers spaced properly during the shift; **do not let your hand collapse**.

In order to play the notes at the fourth and fifth frets, we will need to shift the hand position two frets higher on the fingerboard. As a result, your 1st finger will now be on the third fret, your 2nd finger will be on the fourth fret, and your 4th finger will be on the fifth fret.

The 3rd , 4th , and 5th Frets

		3rd Fret	4th Fret	5th Fret	5th Fret	4th Fret	3rd Fret
4th String		G	G♯	A	A	A♭	G
	Fingering:	1	2	4	4	2	1
3rd String		C	C♯	D	D	D♭	C
		1	2	4	4	2	1
2nd String		F	F♯	G	G	G♭	F
		1	2	4	4	2	1
1st String		A♯	B	C	C	B	B♭
		1	2	4	4	2	1

Play the first five notes of the 4th string. Notice that the shift occurs after the F#, allowing G-G#-A to be played under one hand position. A small dash in between finger numberings indicates a shift.

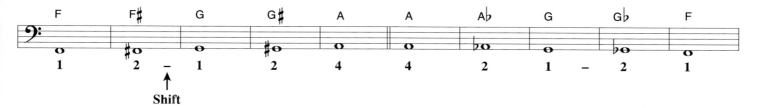

Use the same fingering for the 3rd, 2nd, and 1st strings

Exercise #1

Exercise #2

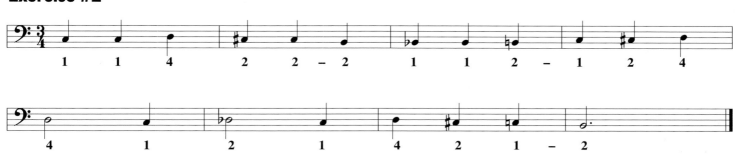

Exercise #3

Exercise #4

Connecting All Four Strings – Shifting

Be sure to follow the fingerings and shifts provided.

Billy Boy

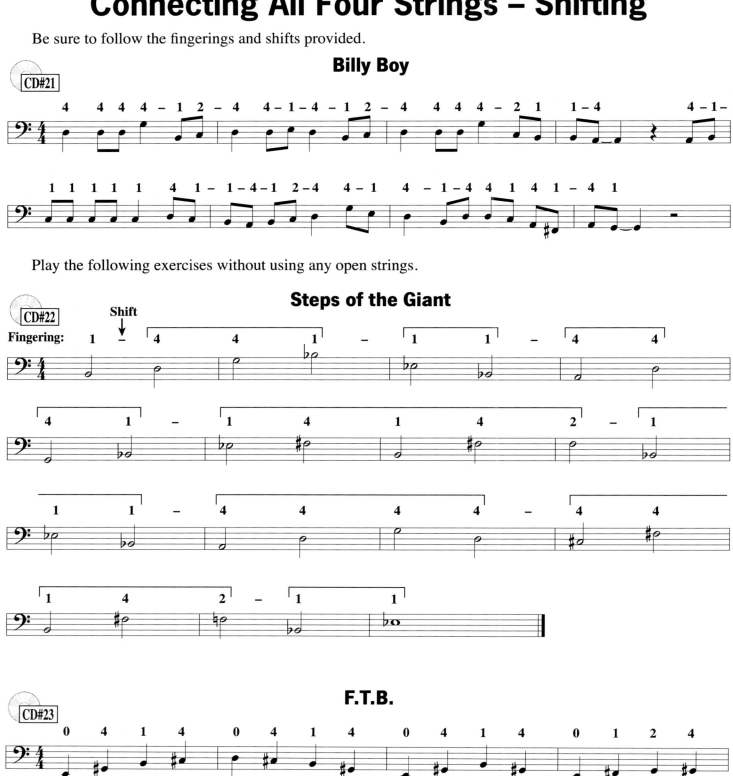

Play the following exercises without using any open strings.

Steps of the Giant

F.T.B.

Advancing Up the Fingerboard

You have probably noticed by now that there is often more than one position to find any given note. For example, the note A at the fifth fret on the 4th string is the same as open A. In both cases, the note is written in the same place in the staff; the choice of which "A" to play is up to the player. The fact that the same note can be located at two different positions may seem confusing at first, but if you take some time to study the layout of the fingerboard you will see certain patterns develop. You will find that these different note locations will help you to navigate your way around the higher positions of the fingerboard.

Always try to group as many notes in one hand position as possible to avoid unnecessary shifts.

The following example is fingered two different ways:

The second fingering is preferable because all the notes may be played without shifting.

The 5ᵗʰ, 6ᵗʰ and 7ᵗʰ Frets

	5th Fret	6th Fret	7th Fret	7th Fret	6th Fret	5th Fret
4th String	A	A♯	B	B	B♭	A
3rd String	D	D♯	E	E	E♭	D
2nd String	G	G♯	A	A	A♭	G
1st String	C	C♯	D	D	D♭	C

Go back to the exercises on pages 20 & 21 and play them starting at the fifth fret instead of using open strings. Notice the that half step and whole step relationship between the notes stays the same even though you are playing in a different part of the fingerboard. You will need to adjust some of the fingerings since you have eliminated open strings. Remember, try and accommodate as many notes under one hand position as possible.

Bass Line Essentials

Now that you are getting comfortable with the feel and sound of the bass, let's look at the role the bass plays in a musical group.

Listen to some of your favorite recordings and try to identify the different instruments being used in each song. Each instrument in a musical group or ensemble has a specific function. Instruments such as the saxophone, trumpet, vocals, or guitar play melodies. A **melody** is a succession of individual notes. Instruments such as the keyboard or guitar play chords. A **chord** is formed when 3 or more notes are played at the same time. Instruments such as the electric or acoustic bass play the **bass line**. If you think of a piece of music in terms of layers, the melody is the top layer, the chords are in the middle and the bass line is the bottom layer.

Bass lines provide a solid foundation for a chord by emphasizing the root of that chord. ***The letter name of a chord determines the root of the chord***. For example, the note "G" is the root of any G chord (major, minor, diminished, etc.), "G♯" is the root of any G♯ chord, and "B♭" is the root of any B♭ chord.

A chord symbol is usually an upper case letter that appears above a measure. Sometimes other symbols appear with the letter. These symbols do not change the root of the chord. A predetermined series of chords is called a chord progression.

Sample Chord Progression

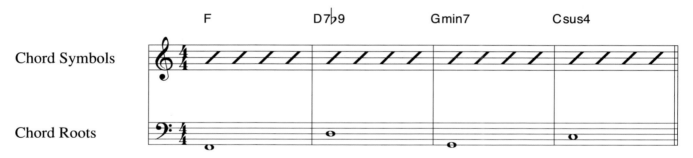

Rhythm

Another important function of a bass line is to provide a strong rhythmic foundation; in other words, a bass player must be able to groove! Diligent practice with a metronome will help you to establish a strong sense of time. Be sure to practice all the exercises, melodies, and bass lines presented in this book with a metronome. Also, listen to recordings of good bass players. Try to identify the rhythmic patterns used to establish a solid groove. You can learn a great deal about how to play great bass lines by listening to great bass players.

The Blues Progression

The blues chord progression is very common in many popular styles of music including blues, rock, pop, and country. A normal blues chord progression is 12 measures long and uses three different chords. A blues bass line outlines the chords in the progression and is often very repetitive.

The following blues progression is in the *key of G*. The first chord of the blues progression determines the key of the blues. The bass line uses all quarter notes; this is called a "walking" style bass line. This bass line is built on an 8-note pattern which lasts for 8 beats or two full measures.

Blues Progression in G

Notice the relationship between the bass line and the chords. The first note of the pattern is always the root of the chord. The first chord, "G", lasts for 4 measures. The 8-note pattern is played 2 times, starting on the note G in the first measure and the third measure.

Measures 1–4

The second chord, "C", appears is measures 5 and lasts for two measures. The pattern is started on the note C in measure 5 and is played once. The "G" chord returns in measure 7 and lasts for two measures. The pattern is started on the note G and is played once.

Measures 5–8

The third chord, "D", appears in measure 9 and lasts for one measure. Starting on the note D, only the first 4 notes of the pattern is played to accommodate the 4 beat duration of the "D" chord. The "C" chord returns in the next measure (measure 10) and lasts for one measure. Again, only the first four notes of the pattern are played to accommodate the 4 beat duration of the "C" chord.

Measures 9–10

The "G" chord returns for the final two measures (measures 11 and 12). The pattern is played one time starting on the note G.

Measures 11–12

Blues Bass Line #2

Using the same blues progression as before, this bass line is built on a 4-note pattern; the first note is always the root of the chord. The eighth notes are played in a "shuffle" style.

Other Blues Bass Line Patterns

28

Play each pattern in the G blues progression. Use CD#25 for each pattern.

You have probably noticed a pattern in the movement of the three chords in the blues progression. This pattern stays the same for any key; likewise, the bass line patterns stay the same. To play a blues in the key of A, simply start the bass line pattern on the note A and follow the chord pattern. The chords are provided below in the form of a *chord chart*. The bass line is not written out; the bass player is free to play any bass line that fits the style. Choose one of the patterns you have learned. The slashes in the measures indicate the beats.

Blues Progression in A

CD#26

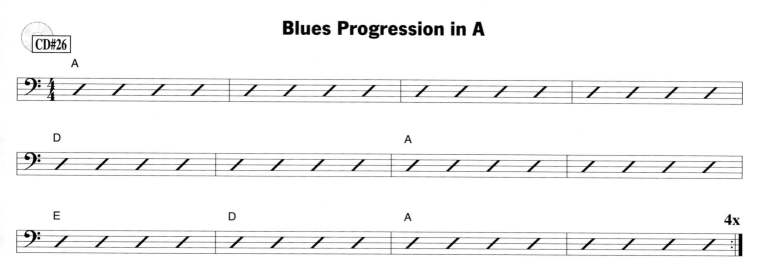

Moving a chord progression, bass line, or melody from one key to another is called *transposing*.

Transpose the blues progression to the key of B♭ and play all 6 blues patterns in the new key.

Blues Progression in B♭

CD#27

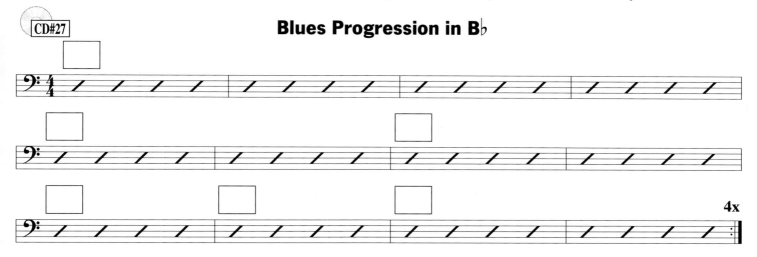

29

The Root–Fifth Relationship

Many bass lines are built around two notes: the *root* (◆) and the *fifth* of the chord being played. We have already discussed how to find the root of a chord; the fifth is located 3 1/2 steps above the root. For example, to find a fifth above the root note C, count up 3 1/2 steps (C-D-E-F#-G) to the note G.

On the bass, the **fifth above** the root is always located two frets higher than the root on an adjacent **higher string**. The root is played with 1st finger; the fifth is played with 4th finger:

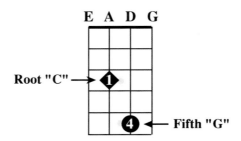

The **fifth below** the root is always located on the same fret on the adjacent **lower string.** Both the root and the fifth are played with first finger:

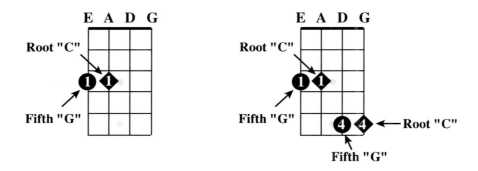

The following bass line alternates between the root and fifth of each chord change.

Boom–Chuck

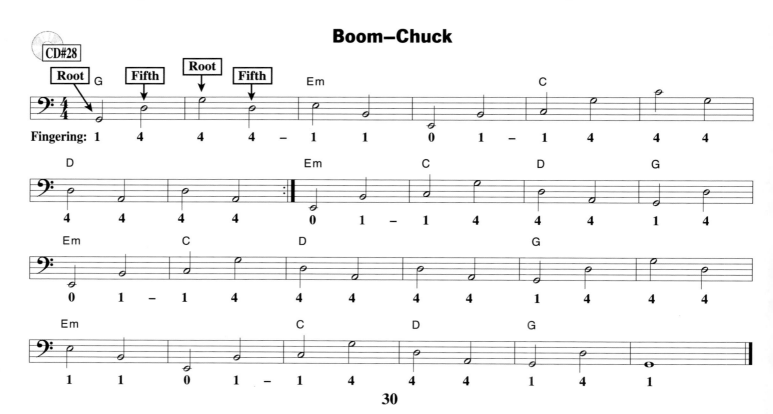

30

The Dotted Quarter Note

A quarter note's value is increased by one-half when a dot is placed to the right of a quarter note.

The dotted quarter note lasts for a beat and a half:

Compare the placement of the dotted quarter note with steady eighth notes.

The "*dotted quarter + eighth note*" rhythm shown above is used often in the bass lines of many different styles of music.

Bass Lines Using "Dotted Quarter + Eighth Note" Rhythms

Green 182

Latin Blues

This bass line combines the "dotted quarter note + eighth note" rhythm with the alternating root-fith motion.

The Final

The following bass line uses everything you have learned so far: Using a proper left hand position, reading notes and rhythms in bass clef notation, and applying a functional bass to a chord progression.

In Conclusion...

You now know everything there is to know about playing the electric bass… well maybe not everything, but you are off to a great start. Once you have mastered the fundamentals presented in this book the fun really begins because you can apply everything you learned to the music that is near and dear to your heart. Whether you are into alternative, metal, country, blues, or punk the same principles apply to bass lines of all styles of music. Put on a CD of your favorite band and try to play along. Listen to the bass line and determine its character. Is it using fast notes, long notes, low notes, high notes? Are there any patterns being repeated? This may seem impossible at first, but with a little time and effort your ability to play what you hear will improve. Finally, take what you have learned out into the world! Communicating through music is a very exciting and rewarding experience. Find some other musicians to play with and experiment with creating your own music. Have fun!